GW01326100

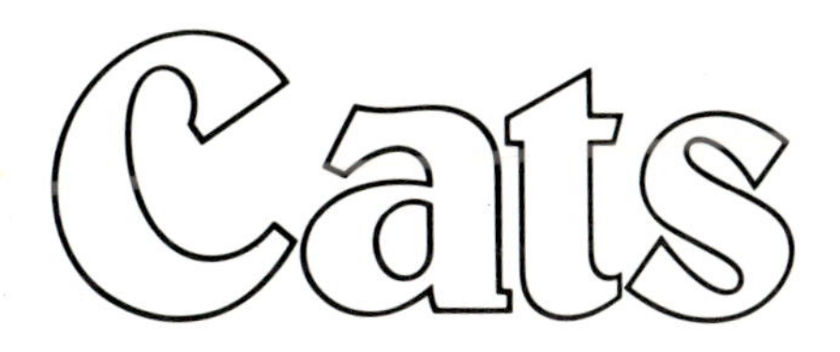

Christine Butterworth and Donna Bailey

MACMILLAN

This is my cat.

Her name is Tess.

Tess likes to play with me.
Then she has her dinner.

Tess has two dishes.
She has meat or fish in one dish.
She has milk or water in
the other dish.

Tess chews her cat biscuits.
They keep her teeth strong and clean.

Tess eats grass too.
Grass keeps her well and
makes her fur shine.

Tess cleans her fur every day.
She licks it with her tongue.

When Tess is angry she wags her tail.
She puts out her sharp claws
and spits.

Tess sharpens her claws on trees.
She can catch rats and
mice with her sharp claws.

Tess is getting very fat.
Soon she will have some kittens.

Tess makes a nest in a box.
She lies in the box when
her kittens are born.

Now Tess has four little kittens.
They are blind but they can crawl.

Tess is a good mother.
She cleans her kittens and
feeds them with her milk.

Now the kittens are two weeks old.

Their eyes are open.

When Tess wants to move her kittens
she carries them gently in her mouth.

Now the kittens are six weeks old.
They can climb out of the box.
They like to play with me.

Now the kittens are much bigger.
It is time for them to go
to new homes.
I kept one kitten to play with Tess.
I gave the others to my friends.

Many people like cats.
They have cats at home as pets.

Some people take their cats to shows.
Some cats win prizes at cat shows.

Farmers keep cats on their farms.
The cats kill the rats that
eat the corn.

Some cats are wild.
They hunt for their own food.

These wild cats live in
the mountains of Scotland.

Wild cats sleep during the day.
They hunt at night.
All cats see well in the dark.

There are many wild cats at the zoo.
Most of them are very big.

Lions are very big cats.
They live in Africa.

Tigers are big cats that
live in India.

The stripes on the tiger's coat
help it to hide in the grass.

Leopards like to climb trees.
The spots on the leopard's coat
help it to hide in the tree.

Cheetahs are smaller than leopards.
They can run faster than
a hundred kilometres an hour.

The puma is as big as a leopard.
Some people call it the mountain lion.

This cat is a snow leopard.
It lives in high mountains.
The snow leopard's white fur
helps it to hide in the snow.

There are many different
kinds of cats.
Which cats do you like best?

Reading consultant: Diana Bentley
Editorial consultant: Donna Bailey

Illustrated by Gill Tomblin
Picture research by Suzanne Williams
Designed by Richard Garratt Design

This edition specially produced for
Macmillan Children's Books,
a division of Macmillan Publishers Limited

First published 1988

This edition published by
Macmillan Children's Books,
a division of Macmillan Publishers Limited
4 Little Essex Street, London WC2R 3LF and Basingstoke
Associated companies throughout the world.

Printed in Hong Kong

British Library Cataloguing in Publication Data
Butterworth, Christine
Cats.——(My world).
1. Cats——Juvenile literature
I. Title II. Bailey, Donna III. Series
636.8 SF445.7
ISBN 0-333-45954-7

All photographs by Peter Greenland except:
Cover: ZEFA
Animal Photography: 19 (R. Willbie)
Bruce Coleman: 18, 21, 22 & 23 (Hans Reinhard), 25 (Jen & Des Bartlett), 26 (Alain Compost), 27 (Peter Jackson), 28 & 29 (Philip Kahl), 30 (Stephen J. Krasemann)
Frank Lane Picture Agency: 31 (Terry Whittaker)
ZEFA: 20